SELF-CHECK

by JaNeise Sturdivant

Self-Check copyright © July 2020 by JaNeise Sturdivant

All rights reserved. No part of this publication may be reproduced, stored in a retrieval system, or transmitted in any form by any means, electronic, mechanical, photocopy, recording, or otherwise, without the prior permission of the publisher, except as provided for by USA copyright law.

ISBN: 978-1-7352672-0-3
LCCN: 2020911658

Published by Maximized Productions, LLC.
UPH Publishing Div.
6715 Suitland Rd., Morningside, MD 20746
www.maximizedproductions.com
Cover Design: Maximized Productions, LLC.
UPH Pub. Div.
Book Design by Dawn M. Harvey

Please direct your inquiries to the email address below or visit:
jsturdivant2@gmail.com or http://www.jesienmdmgt.com/
PRINTED IN THE UNITED STATES OF AMERICA

INTRODUCTION

The purpose of life is to live a life of purpose. Being uncertain of one's self, or one's existence, will make it difficult to fulfill one's purpose. There is an order to this.

I pray that this journey of self-discovery will help you to gain Your-Self with knowing how to discover your purpose for your life and to help YOU embrace YOU so that one day you can tell your own story the way it was meant to be told!

A famous saying: *"Never let people's thoughts about you hinder you from accomplishing what God has put in your heart. Dare to dream and dare to live it!"*

ACKNOWLEDGEMENTS:

First and foremost, Praise and Thanks to God, the Almighty, for His showers of blessings through this journey. I am thankful to God for giving me the strength and power to believe in my passion and pursue my dreams.

It is the gift of time, support, and love that Mentors provide to individuals that help make the world a better place; I am grateful to be amongst the chosen to provide this gift into future leaders.

Thank you to everyone who strives to grow and help others grow. It is the business version of The Lion King song "Circle of Life."

To all individuals I have had the opportunity to lead, be led by, or watch their leadership from afar, I want to say thank you for being the inspiration and foundation for Self-Check.

Having an idea and turning it into a book is as hard as it sounds. This experience was both internally challenging and rewarding. I especially want to thank the individuals that helped make this happen. Without the experiences and support from my parents, Pastor J.E and Lady P.D. Sturdivant, my family, my mentor, and my peers, this book would not exist. I am extremely grateful for all of your love, prayers, caring, and sacrifice with educating and preparing me for my future.

Finally, I wish to thank everyone on my publishing team at Maximized Productions, for your support and assistance in contributing to the success of the creation of my first book.

TABLE OF CONTENTS

SECTION ONE: SELF-CONFIDENCE

Part I: Who Am I? 2

Part II: WHO DO YOU BELIEVE? 6

Part III: Do I Really Believe? 9

SECTION TWO: SELF-CARE

Part I: Got Balance? 15

Part II: Just Say No 18

Part III: Just Say Yes 21

SECTION THREE: SELF-ESTEEM

Part I: Choices 28

Part II: Healthy vs. Unhealthy Relationships...31

Part III: Growth Within..37

SECTION FOUR: SELF-WORTH

Part I: Beyond Value..43

Part II: The Heart of the Matter..46

Part III: Positive Regard...49

SECTION FIVE: SELF- LOVE

Part I: Priceless 57

Part II: Boundaries..60

Part III: Accepting You 64

SECTION ONE: SELF-CONFIDENCE

SELF-CONFIDENCE IS A FEELING OF TRUST IN ONE'S ABILITIES, QUALITIES, AND JUDGEMENT

PART I: WHO AM I?

Have you ever asked yourself, 'Who am I really?' By not knowing the answer to the question, 'Who am I?', you keep on creating new identities of yourself, consequently going farther away from your true self. When you say Who am I, allow yourself to be the real you!! Don't allow what people say you can or can't do to dictate who you are; if you don't identify who you are, you're pretending!! Who am I, I am not what you expect me to be, I AM WHO I AM!! All the suffering in life is because of not knowing your true identity; you believe yourself to be the name that has been given to you.

One of the trickiest tasks we ever face is that of working out who we really are. If we're asked directly to describe ourselves, our minds tend to go blank. We can't just sum ourselves up. We need prompts and suggestions and more detailed enquiries that help tease out and organize our picture of ourselves.

Confidence is feeling emotionally sure, secure, and strong it's the opposite of feeling fearful, anxious, or scared. Self-confidence is by being decisive, trying new things, or staying in control when things get a little difficult; a person with high self-confidence seems to live life with passion and enthusiasm.

ACTIVITY   CREATE A SELF-PORTRAIT

Self-portraits offerpeopleacreativeoutlettoexpresshowtheyviewthemselves.

- How is your portrait different from the image you project to others?

- What is a step you are willing to take to improve your vision of yourself?

- How will you use what you have learned?

CREATE SELF-PORTRAIT

Self-portraits offer people a creative outlet to express how they view themselves.

ACTIVITY PAGE

- How is your portrait different from the image you project to others?

_____

_____

_____

_____

- What is a step you are willing to take to improve your vision of yourself?

_____

_____

_____

_____

- How will you use what you have learned?

_____

_____

_____

_____

SCRIPTURE

"But you are a chosen race, a royal priesthood, a holy nation, a people for his own possession, that you may proclaim the excellencies of him who called you out of darkness into his marvelous light." 1 Peter 2:9

PART II: WHO DO YOU BELIEVE?

Self-confidence is "a way of being in the world that allows you to know yourself and to take care of yourself." Being aware of when you are struggling and having the strength to commit to doing something about it.

Ultimately, without self-confidence, we condemn ourselves to a life of servitude of doing what we believe and doing what we're told instead of us doing what we really believe is right. Without confidence, we condemn ourselves to a life in servitude of those who have it.

Reasons for the point:

- **SOCIAL**- Nothing feels better or stings harder than feedback from others. This means your successes must be witnessed. Start in private, by all means, but know that the greatest leaps in self-worth will come from victories that are "known."

- **EFFORT**- The wonderful thing about trying hard is it almost always succeeds, eventually. I'm not a natural runner, but if I try hard enough, I will accomplish something through sheer force of will, and that breeds self-worth. In the absence of confidence, work your butt off!

- **RESILIENCE**- The most important thing is how you handle knocks. They are inevitable. They will make you feel like crap. But the longer you linger on them, the further your confidence will tumble. Counter swiftly: try again, try something else, but never dwell on the negative.

ACTIVITY- CREATE POSITIVE AFFIRMATIONS EVERYDAY

- Start with the words "I am."

_____
_____

- Use the present tense.

_____
_____

- State it in the positive.

_____
_____

- Keep it brief.

_____
_____

- Make it specific.

_____
_____

SCRIPTURE

"I am the vine; you are the branches. Whoever abides in me and I in him, he it is that bears much fruit, for apart from me you can do nothing."
John 15:5

PART III: DO I REALLY BELIEVE?

So what does it mean to believe in you and possess self-confidence? Loosely defined, it is the feeling of confidence in our judgment, abilities, and qualities. It is sometimes referred to as self-efficacy. This, in turn, affects almost every area of our lives, including how we think, feel, and act. This is why it is so important.

In order to have true self confidence, it is important that we are responsible for everything that makes up the real us, both positive and negative and it should not alter what you really believe. All of us have made mistakes, experienced failure, and felt disappointment in our lives. I know I certainly have had more than my fair share. Some of us have also been subjected to hardships and injustices. All these experiences affect a person's self-confidence and faith in his or her own abilities. Fortunately, there are ways to develop a strong self-belief even though it does require some time and effort. It is important to remember that our past does not have to dictate our future. The only thing that matters is how we act today.

There are many factors that affect our self-confidence, including our parents, our upbringing, our environment, our beliefs, past failures and successes, society, how other people treat us, the media, and our experiences at large. Research suggests that the beliefs individuals hold about their abilities powerfully influence the ways in which they behave and achieve. Interestingly enough, a lack of self-confidence is not directly related to a lack of talent, skill or ability. It is more related to our perception.

ACTIVITY – CREATE A LIST OF YOUR PAST SUCCESSES, ACCOMPLISHMENTS AND SHORTCOMINGS

List A – Success and Accomplishments (Write Down How Your Learned From Them)

___

___

___

___

___

List B – Shortcomings That Can Be Turned Into Successes (Write Down How Your Learned From Them)

___

___

___

___

___

___

SCRIPTURE

"Or do you not know that your body is a temple of the Holy Spirit within you, whom you have from God? You are not your own, for you were bought with a price. So glorify God in your body."
1 Corinthians 6:19-20

SELF CHECK CHALLENGE

How confident are you? Let's take a quiz

1. Do you like yourself? ___ ☐ YES ☐ NO
2. Do you feel lonely most of the time? ___ ☐ YES ☐ NO
3. Do you want to look different? ___ ☐ YES ☐ NO
4. Do you take full responsibility for your actions? ___ ☐ YES ☐ NO
5. Do you compare yourself to others? ___ ☐ YES ☐ NO
6. Are you concerned about what others say about yourself? ___ ☐ YES ☐ NO
7. Do you feel comfortable attending to a party? ___ ☐ YES ☐ NO
8. Do you focus on your failures instead of your successes? ___ ☐ YES ☐ NO
9. Do you think that you are worthy to be loved? ___ ☐ YES ☐ NO
10. Do you blame others often? ___ ☐ YES ☐ NO
11. Do you blame yourself often? ___ ☐ YES ☐ NO
12. Do you always finish what you started? ___ ☐ YES ☐ NO
13. Do you need recognition to feel good about yourself? ___ ☐ YES ☐ NO
14. Are you confident all the time? ___ ☐ YES ☐ NO
15. Do you stand up for yourself? ___ ☐ YES ☐ NO
16. Do you think that you are talented? ___ ☐ YES ☐ NO
17. Do you have goals or dreams to accomplish? ___ ☐ YES ☐ NO
18. Do you give before you get? ___ ☐ YES ☐ NO
19. Do you tell the truths to yourself? ___ ☐ YES ☐ NO
20. Do you think you can handle any situations? ___ ☐ YES ☐ NO
21. Do you like being alone sometimes? ___ ☐ YES ☐ NO
22. Do you always achieve your goals? ___ ☐ YES ☐ NO

Score: If you answered YES to the following questions give yourself "1" point after each answer;

1, 4, 7, 9, 12, 14-22. The answer NO equals "O" point.

If you answered YES to the following questions give yourself "O" point after each answer;

2, 3, 5, 6, 8, 10, 11, 13. The answer NO equals "1" point.

The higher the score the higher the level of your self-confident.

MIRROR MOMENT

Every day take 5 minutes and list positive traits about yourself, something that you don't like about yourself, and what you can do to change it.

_____
_____
_____
_____
_____
_____
_____
_____
_____
_____
_____
_____
_____
_____
_____

SECTION TWO: SELF-CARE

SELF-CARE IS THE ACCEPTANCE OF PERSONAL RESPONSIBILITY LEADING TOWARD GETTING FILLED MENTALLY, PHYSICALLY, SPIRITUALLY AND EMOTIONALLY

PART I: GOT BALANCE?

"How do I find my balance in life?" Balancing school, family, a social life, physical needs, and mental health is not easy. To have a healthy approach to your life, you need to work on your identity outside of school, work, family, etc. Start by paying attention to what you pay attention to.

It is possible to be both productive and relaxed. We have a mental, physical and emotional identity, as well as a psychic. Each of these areas requires attention and care, but generally we can think of ourselves in two ways: we have inner needs that must be met, and we have outer responsibilities that must be attended to.

The key to living better is balancing all aspects of work, play and self-care, and remaining happy, healthy and vibrant is possible by attending to the mind, body and heart centers. Be compassionate and kind to yourself and others as you work, play and take care of yourself.

I find it so helpful to take a day (or even a few hours) to myself to truly assess my life and goals. I use this time to reflect on the past and plan for the future. It's one of my most important self-care routines!

I hope you gain a fresh perspective on your life from taking the self-care assessment. The results should really help you find where you need to improve your self-care routines. Please share in the comments below what you have discovered about yourself!

ACTIVITY- EXERCISE

Intense exercise for two to five minutes a day. Exercising for a short period will help your body get rid of negative energy. Try walking at a fast pace, doing jumping jacks, etc. Exercise help combat any uncomfortable emotions like anger, anxiety, or sadness.

SCRIPTURE

"Beloved, I pray that you may prosper in all things and be in health, just as your soul prospers." 3 John 1:2

PART II- JUST SAY NO

It's easy to fall into the habit of saying "yes," but when it imposes on your well-being, sometimes it is better to say "no."

While many of us have discovered that helping others is one of the best parts of life, learning how to say no when you're overburdened (or getting there) is a great self-care tool that you can learn. We all face fears about saying no, fears about hurting feelings and being disliked; and some of us have never learned how to say no based on our childhoods or roles growing up.

Here's how to say no with less stress and guilt, it really can be this simple:

1. Just Say "I'm Sorry, Can't Do This Right Now"- It's OK to just repeat, "I'm sorry, but this just doesn't fit into my schedule," and change the subject, or even walk away if you have to.

2. Give Yourself Time - This gives you a chance to review your schedule, as well as your feelings about saying "yes" to another commitment, do a cost-benefit analysis, and then get back to them with a yes or no. Most importantly, this tactic helps you avoid letting yourself be pressured into over scheduling your life and taking on too much stress.

3. Say Yes to Something Else - Mention a lesser commitment that you can make; this way you'll still be partially involved, but it will be on your own terms.

When saying "no" Be Firm, Be Clear, and No Excuses Necessary.

ACTIVITY - PRACTICE GRATITUDE:

One simple way to practice gratitude is by writing down 3 things you're grateful for everyday. Remembering to find things, experiences, and people in your life that you're grateful for can have powerful effects on your mood.

SCRIPTURE

"Do not conform to the pattern of this world, but be transformed by the renewing of your mind. Then you will be able to test what God's will is: his good, pleasing and perfect will." Romans 12:2

PART III – JUST SAY YES

If you have not learned how to give yourself appropriate doses of self-care, running on "empty" and resisting taking care of yourself may be common. As a result, your nerves can get frazzled and you feel overloaded most of the time.

Learning that you have personal needs, which require attention and renewal is very difficult for many of us. As a child, you may have heard: "Don't be selfish." You may have taken this phrase into teenage and adulthood and confused essential self-care with selfishness.

You don't call your cell phone selfish for having little juice left in its battery. Instead, you immediately find the closest charger. Yet "selfish" is what you may call yourself when you need recharging.

Maintaining a daily self-care practice, just a few minutes at a time, of intentionally acknowledging your needs and what you care about, is best. Gradually you will notice you feel better and able to weather the moments of daily drama when they arise. A sustainable self-care practice is about creating a clear intention to support and love you.

ACTIVITY - DAILY MEDITATION

A five-minute routine using a technique that mentally and emotionally brings clarity, calm and a stable state.

SCRIPTURE

"And now, dear brothers and sisters, one final thing. Fix your thoughts on what is true, and honorable, and right, and pure, and lovely, and admirable. Think about things that are excellent and worthy of praise." Philippians 4:8

SELF CHECK CHALLENGE

Self-Care Assessment

Using the scale below, rate the following areas in terms of frequency:

5 = Frequently 4 = Occasionally 3 = Rarely 2 = Never 1 = It never occurred to me

Physical Self-Care

- Eat regularly (e.g. breakfast, lunch and dinner)
- Eat healthy
- Exercise
- Get regular medical care for prevention
- Get medical care when needed
- Take time off when needed
- Get massages
- Dance, swim, walk, run, play sports, sing, or do some other physical activity that is fun
- Get enough sleep
- Wear clothes you like
- Take vacations
- Take day trips or mini-vacations
- Make time away from telephones

Emotional Self-Care

- Spend time with others whose company you enjoy
- Stay in contact with important people in your life
- Give yourself affirmations; praise yourself
- Love yourself
- Re-read favorite books, re-view favorite movies
- Identify comforting activities, objects, people, relationships, places and seek them out
- Allow yourself to cry
- Find things that make you laugh
- Express your outrage in social action, letters and donations, marches, protests
- Play with children

Spiritual Self-Care

- Make time for reflection
- Find a spiritual connection or community
- Be open to inspiration
- Identify what is meaningful to you
- Meditate
- Pray
- Sing
- Spend time with love ones
- Contribute to causes in which you believe
- Read inspirational literature (talks, music, etc.)

MIRROR MOMENT

Everyday do something you love: Carve out time for your passions and hobbies, whether that's hiking, crafting, dancing, reading for fun, etc. Hobbies can provide you an outlet for managing stress and can increase happiness levels.

SECTION THREE: SELF-ESTEEM

SELF-ESTEEM ENCOMPASSES BELIEFS ABOUT ONESELF AS WELL AS ONE'S

PART I: CHOICES

Self-esteem is a subjective image that we hold inside of us, that represent our beliefs about who we are, our abilities, and our worth. It is our own view of ourselves, it may not be accurate or how others view us, but it affects every aspect of our lives. Whether or not our self-esteem is positive or negative will have great effect on how we think, how we communicate, our relationships, our careers, and our goals for the future.

There are simple, everyday conscious choices that we can make to improve our self-esteem and help build a healthy perspective on ourselves and our self-worth. When you focus on others and support them, you will find that it is also therapeutic for you and your situation. Finding out about your abilities and adjustments when placed in unfamiliar situations greatly enhances your self-esteem – PUSH OUTSIDE YOUR COMFORT ZONE!

Self-esteem is made up of your self-confidence and your self-respect.

Self-confidence, meaning that you're confident in your ability to think, learn, decide, and respond to change.

Self-respect, meaning that you think success, achievement, fulfillment, and happiness are what you naturally deserve.

Your self-esteem is the most important asset you have, and it should be treated that way. It should be strengthened and nurtured constantly and daily.

SCRIPTURE

"I praise you because I am fearfully and wonderfully made; your works are wonderful, I know that full well." Psalm 139:14

ACTIVITY PAGE

What are three words that describe you?

1. _____

2. _____

3. _____

What are three words your friends would use to describe you?

1. _____

2. _____

3. _____

What are your values (things that are important to you)?

1. _____

2. _____

3. _____

PART II- HEALTHY VS. UNHEALTHY RELATIONSHIPS

Self-esteem affects your relationships, and the reverse is true also. By strengthening one's self-esteem, one will increase contentment in relationships and, as a result, the emotional health of all family members. Positive self-esteem is critical to an individual's mental health and ability to relate well to others. Low self-esteem will affect your relationships negatively; it may make you attract negative people into your life.

If you have low self-esteem, there's a possibility that you won't be able to relate to well with others. You may feel a lack of confidence in social situations. Your body language may be negative and you will not respond to others positively.

If you do not behave confidently, others may take advantage of this by criticizing you and making you feel worse. Your manner is likely to make others respond coldly and this will damage your relationship with others.

How can you build your self-esteem and improve your relationships?

You can take steps each day to build confidence and feel better about yourself. Let's look at a few of the most important steps you can take to build your self-esteem:

1. Understand that the way someone treats you says more about the other person than it does about you. If a person is abusive or mistreats you, it shows that they have a problem. Maybe they are angry at the world or angry at themselves and are taking it out on you. They need help to sort this out.

2. Often by feeling rejected you will do the same and reject others and maybe go as far as rejecting everything in your life, even yourself. To change this you need to look for what is good about you and your life and focus on those things. This change will mean you'll stop rejecting and encouraging others to reject you.

3. Probably the best thing you can do today to help yourself build self-esteem and confidence is to accept who you are and understand what makes you unique. Ask yourself: "What talents and strengths do I have?" When you understand that there is so much good inside you and that you are a uniquely gifted person, then you will feel so much better about who you are. This will enable you to face the world more positively and your relationships will reflect this amazing change.

ACTIVITY - A LETTER TO YOURSELF

Write four letters to your future self detailing whatever you wish, whether it details your life and relationships at the moment or future goals. Revisit your letter in the workbook in three months and then revise the letter every three months. After a year, read all four letters to see how much you've changed.

A LETTER TO MY FUTURE SELF

A LETTER TO MY FUTURE SELF

A LETTER TO MY FUTURE SELF

SCRIPTURE

"This is my command- be strong and courageous! Do not be afraid or discouraged. For the Lord your God is with you wherever you go." Joshua 1:9

PART III- GROWTH WITHIN

The way you view yourself, your perceptions, and your beliefs about who you are and what you're capable of doing all depend on your self-esteem. Self-esteem has little to do with talent or abilities, but it is the cornerstone of personal growth.

In the process of exploring your talents, there's nothing you can do but face the worst of your fears: YOURSELF! Your self-image is linked to your limitations, your past, your wounds, your particular way of being. Doubts about whether you'll fit in, whether you'll be able to do something or not, or whether what you drag along in your emotional backpack will keep you from moving forward and these doubts are scary.

Only by daring to be yourself, accepting who you are, and loving yourself unconditionally, will you be able to start to heal your self-esteem and, as a result, be in a position to fulfill your potential.

Make peace with yourself, and it will free you from the limitations you impose on yourself or accept from other people. Making peace with yourself involves accepting those weaknesses and relying on them to take the first step towards personal growth.

What other people think doesn't concern you. Nobody can please everybody. Trying to satisfy everybody is a fruitless effort, especially if you forget that the first person who should be proud of your actions is yourself. Don't forget that many people only see a limited version of you. Nobody can know your motives, your goals, your efforts better than you.

Grow so that you can get past other people's judgments and see yourself the way you are and the way you want to be.

ACTIVITY – MEDITATE

Set aside time each day to remove stress in your mind and body and release negative thoughts and energy by casting your cares and talking to God about what you are feeling.

_____

_____

_____

_____

_____

_____

_____

_____

_____

_____

_____

_____

_____

SCRIPTURE

"But when he came to himself,... I will arise and go" Luke 15: 17, 18

SELF CHECK CHALLENGE

Self- esteem checkup

Directions: Rate from 0 to 10 how much you believe each statement. "O" Means you do not believe it at all and "10" Means you completely believe in it.

1. I believe in myself _____

2. I am just as valuable as other people _____

3. I would rather be me then someone else _____

4. I am proud of my accomplishments _____

5. I feel good when I get compliments _____

6. I can handle criticism _____

7. I am good at solving problems _____

8. I love trying new things _____

9. I respect myself _____

10. I like the way I look _____

11. I Love myself even when others reject me _____

12. I know my positive qualities _____

13. I focus on my successes and not my failures _____

14. I'm not afraid to made mistakes _____

15. I am happy to be _____

Overall, how would you rate your self-esteem on the following scale?

0_____10

MIRROR MOMENT

Listing Traits

Every week simply make a list of your positive character traits that make you a good friend, good sister/brother, and child. Describe in detailed scenarios that describe how you fit those positive traits/titles.

SECTION FOUR: SELF-WORTH

THE SENSE OF ONE'S OWN VALUE OR WORTH AS A PERSON

PART I- BEYOND VALUE

Self-worth may be a less-popular research topic than self-esteem or self-confidence, but that doesn't mean it's less important. Self-worth is at the core of our very selves, our thoughts, feelings, and behaviors are intimately tied into how we view our worthiness and value as human beings. Your self-worth is determined mostly by your self-evaluated abilities and your performance in one or more activities that you deem valuable.

Most people measure their self-worth to others by the following:

- Appearance- the size of clothing worn, or the kind of attention received by others

- Net worth- this can mean income, material possessions, and financial assets

- Who you know/your social circle- some people judge their own value and the value of others by their status and what important people they know

- What you do/your career- we often judge others by what they do

- What you achieve- we frequently use achievements/success to determine someone's worth (whether it's our own worth or someone else's)

One of the most common mistakes you see people with low self-esteem make is to base their self-worth on one aspect of their life, for example, a relationship. It is important work on feeling good about yourself whether you are in a relationship or not. The love of another person does not define you, nor does it define your value as a person. Whether you are single or not, you are worthy of love and respect, and you should make time to practice self-acceptance and self-compassion. Society will dictate your self-worth according to the above; but your superior thoughts should control your self-worth. ONLY YOU HAVE THE ABILITY TO DO OR NOT DO!

ACTIVITY- ENHANCE YOUR SELF-LOVE

To boost self-love, start paying attention to the tone you use with yourself. Commit to being more positive and uplifting when talking to yourself.

Every day, think (or say aloud) these simple statements:

- I feel valued and special

- I love myself wholeheartedly

- I am a worthy and capable person

SCRIPTURE

"The Lord will perfect that which concerns me; your mercy, O Lord, endures forever; Do not forsake the works of Your hands."
Psalms 138:8

PART II: THE HEART OF THE MATTER

One way in which we gain a healthy sense of self-worth is through early and frequent experiences of success. Successful experiences boost our sense of competency and mastery and make us feel just plain good about ourselves.

Showing unconditional love or unconditional respect and positive regard is the best way to teach self-worth. To increase self-worth, look back at what does not determine self-worth. Remind yourself that your bank account, job title, attractiveness, and social media following have nothing to do with how valuable or worthy a person you are.

It's easy to get caught up in chasing money, status, and popularity, especially when these things are highly valued by those around us and by society in general, but make an effort to take a step back and think about what truly matters when determining worth: kindness, compassion, empathy, respect for others, and how well we treat those around us.

It is also important to work on identifying, challenging, and externalizing your critical inner voice. We all have an inner critic that loves to nitpick and point out our flaws. It's natural to let this inner critic get the best of us sometimes, but if we let him/her win too often it starts to think that it's right!

When you learn to love yourself, you become better able to love someone else. People with high self-respect tend to have more satisfying, loving, and stable relationships than those who do not, precisely because they know that they need to first find their worth, esteem, and happiness within themselves.

ACTIVITY- RECOGNIZE YOUR SELF-WORTH

Once you understand, accept, and love yourself, you will reach a point where you no longer depend on people, accomplishments, or other external factors for your self-worth.

Daily remind and say to yourself that:

- You no longer need to please other people

- No matter what people do or say and regardless of what happens outside of you, you alone control how you feel about yourself

- You have the power to respond to events and circumstances based on your internal sources, resources, and resourcefulness, which are the reflection of your true value

- Your value comes from inside, from an internal measure that you've set for yourself

SCRIPTURE

"I can do all this through him who gives me strength." Philippians 4:13

PART III: POSITIVE REGARD

Self-worth = You matter!!! You don't matter because you compare favorably to other people or because you meet some measure of good performance. You have value simply because you are you. Self-worth comes from within to give you the ability to receive self-esteem. Self-worth is when you're becoming the best you that you can be; the only competition you have is yourself.

When you value yourself no matter what circumstance you're in or who is around you, you can have what you need and more. You can be your best and do your best. You can have the best quality of life possible for you at any given moment.

Once you find healthy self-worth within yourself, you can reason out your decision and make the best possible choice. You can decide whether a low-risk, medium-risk or high-risk option is best in this specific situation. You don't hesitate to decide or put the decision off on someone else. You know that however it turns out, your life will still matter. You know even if hindsight later reveals you made a mistake, what you decide now is the best decision you can make at this time.

Self-worth is a beautiful thing! Now, how can you improve it? It takes some effort and possibly some additional help to make this change. Here are a few possibilities for increasing your self-worth:

1. **Use Affirmations the Best Way for You**- Positive affirmations can be very helpful tools. The right way to use affirmations when you're starting out with low self-worth is to make them positive but believable to you.

2. **Do What You Love**- Don't put aside what you want to do; know that what matters to you is also important enough to spend your life doing it.

3. **Stop Criticizing Yourself**- Remember that there's a big difference between identifying areas for improvement and criticizing yourself.

4. **Find The Good In Yourself**- When something bad happens to you, you can rebuild your self-worth by looking for the ways you are good in that role or situation.

5. **Use "I Am" with Care**- When you say, "I am," you put limits on yourself. Sometimes, you define yourself in a very harmful way. Instead of labeling yourself with negative words, try labeling the behavior or thought that's concerning you.

ACTIVITY- BOOST YOUR SELF-ACCEPTANCE

Every day, forgive yourself for anything you've done wrong. Think of any struggles, needs for improvement, mistakes, and bad habits you have, and commit to forgiving yourself and accepting yourself without judgment or excuses.

SCRIPTURE

"For God has not given us a spirit of fear, but of power and of love and of a sound mind."
2 Timothy 1:7

SELF-CHECK CHALLENGE

Self-Worth Experiment

Ask and answer the following questions:

1. What if everything I have was suddenly taken away from me?

   _____

2. What if all I had left was just myself?

   _____

3. How would that make me feel?

   _____

4. What would I actually have that would be of value?

   _____

5. Who I am? I am . . . I am not . . .

   _____

6. How am I?

   _____

7. How am I in the world?

8. How do others see me?

9. How do others speak about me?

10. What key life moments define who I am today?

11. What brings me the most passion, fulfillment, and joy?

12. Where do I struggle most?

13. Where do I need to improve?

14. What fears often hold me back?

___

15. What habitual emotions hurt me?

___

16. What mistakes do I tend to make?

___

17. Where do I tend to consistently let myself down?

___

18. What abilities do I have?

___

19. What am I really good at?

___

MIRROR MOMENT

Remind yourself daily of what you have learned about you and know that you hold the power in your own life. Revel in your well-earned sense of self-worth and make sure to maintain it.

SECTION FIVE: SELF- LOVE

THE LOVE OF SELF: SUCH AS AN APPRECIATION OF ONE'S OWN WORTH OR VIRTUE

PART I: PRICELESS

It all begins with a choice. A choice to begin to see through the eyes of love and understand what needs to be adjusted within yourself. Once we understand what our core issues are and what needs the most love, we are already beginning to heal and love ourselves.

Loving yourself is magical. Self-love is a powerful force that will positively affect every single aspect of your life. No more giving in to your inner-critic; no more listening to that voice telling you that you're not good enough; no more settling for less than you deserve. Self-love empowers you to make healthy decisions that serve you in the highest good.

The antidote for self-love is through compassion. Understanding yourself and having compassion for all pieces of yourself, especially the ones that you'd rather disown and ignore. Awareness allows you to live consciously and understand your triggers. It allows you to self-talk and choose differently so that you do not go down the path to self-destruction.

Accept that this is where you are and understand how you got here. You can't beat yourself up when you realize you have an inner child that is hurting from your upbringing, and this is why you are in the position that you are in today. This is why you may put others' needs before your own. You realize it gives you a sense of self-worth. Self-love is a conscious journey. It doesn't happen overnight. It's important to exhibit patience and non-judgment every step of the way.

Today, choose to love you!!

ACTIVITY – CHANGE YOUR NORM

Every day, step outside of your comfort zone and try something new. It's incredible the feeling you get when you realize you have achieved something you didn't know or think you could do before.

SCRIPTURE

"Therefore, if anyone is in Christ, he is a new creation; old things have passed away; behold, all things have become new." 2 Corinthians 5:17

PART II: BOUNDARIES

The definition of a boundary is subject to multiple interpretations. A boundary is an emotional distance or mindset, a restriction that people place on others, and they are present in all relationships. Setting boundaries tells people how they can treat you. Boundaries are personal, emotional spaces that people learn to impose on others; to preserve the value of self-love. To create an emotional space or place a boundary, is like setting an emotional psychological dividing line between the self and another person.

Internal, personal boundaries protect people from getting emotionally upset just as external boundaries protect the country from invasion. The ability to execute an internal boundary depends on how people value their sense of self, their thoughts, ideas, beliefs, and is dependent on one's ability to have self-love. Set boundaries on what you will stand for and what you won't stand for, which develops who you are. Who you are is determined by what you believe in your character and boundaries are what develops your character.

Tips on Setting Boundaries:

Tip 1: Setting Boundaries is the First Step to Regaining Control of Life

It might seem like learning how to walk again, because this is indeed a new learning experience and change can be scary. It takes courage to face fears, but maybe some of these fears are of the imagination.

Tip 2: Direct Communication is the Key

Misinterpretation or lack of communication turns molehills into mountains. Using clear, simple language in a direct, respectful fashion will make you feel proud, simply because you spoke your peace.

Tip 3: Reflections in the Mirror

Accept yourself and take responsibility for mistakes; we all make them at times in life. No one is perfect! We might not have set out to control, but sometimes it happens. This is not about being right or wrong with anyone; it is just learning how to effectively communicate. Forgive yourself, apologize, and you seriously might get that joyful feeling of not only accepting yourself with making a mistake. This takes real strength and courage. Congratulate yourself on your victory and successes; be your own cheerleader with encouraging and motivating yourself.

ACTIVITY- GRATITUDE

Find something to be grateful for every day; write it down. It's inevitable that you are going to have your down days. It's especially important on these days to find at least one thing you are grateful for as it helps to shift your mind and energy around what's going on.

_____

_____

_____

_____

_____

_____

_____

_____

_____

_____

_____

I AM GRATEFUL FOR:

SCRIPTURE

"Your ears shall hear a word behind you, saying, "This is the way, walk in it," Whenever you turn to the right hand or whenever you turn to the left." Isaiah 30:21

PART III: ACCEPTING YOU

Self-Acceptance is accepting all of you, your talents, beauty, your creativity, the wonderful you. You accept yourself despite your flaws, failures, and limitations. It includes self-forgiveness and overcoming guilt. Instead of comparing yourself to others, both positively and negatively, you appreciate your singular individuality. You feel that you're enough without having to improve yourself.

Self-acceptance works wonders. Once you start accepting yourself, you gradually stop worrying what others think and become more spontaneous and natural. Self-acceptance is what allows you to be authentic. You can finally relax and allow more of the inner, real you to be seen. You'll have no shame or fear of revealing yourself when you accept yourself unconditionally. This is the key to intimacy and spiritual relationships and enables you to accept others.

True self-acceptance is embracing who you are, without any qualifications, conditions, or exceptions. It's not enough to simply embrace the good, valuable, or positive about yourself; to embody true self-acceptance, you must also embrace the less desirable, the negative, and the ugly parts of yourself. First, you must acknowledge that you have undesirable traits and habits before you start your journey to improvement.

Self-acceptance is the key to living a happier life.

ACTIVITY- SELF- TALK

Repeat the following statements to yourself, acknowledge them, and absorb them, and you will be well on your way to self-acceptance and self-love.

- I am a good and caring person and deserve to be treated with respect

- I am capable of achieving success in my life

- There are people who love me and will be there for me when I need them

- I deserve to be happy

- I am allowed to make mistakes and learn from them

SCRIPTURE

"Commit your works to the Lord, and your thoughts will be established." Proverbs 16:3

SELF-CHECK CHALLENGE

Today I Choose…..

My Life is a Choice!

Nearly everything you do in life is a choice. You choose to wake up, take a shower, eat breakfast, brush your hair, get dressed, eat, exercise, treat your family and friends a certain way and so on. You make thousands of choices every day!

Write down all the choices you have made already today … starting with the choice to get out of bed. Reflect on what came from your choices, be it positive or not so positive.

_____

_____

_____

_____

_____

_____

_____

_____

_____

MIRROR MOMENT

Buy something you've always wanted and treat you!

SELF-CHECK
30 DAY JOURNAL

My Daily Journal ____ / ____ / ____

My Daily Journal ____ / ____ / ____

My Daily Journal ____ / ____ / ____

My Daily Journal ____ / _____ / _____

My Daily Journal ____ / ____ / ____

My Daily Journal ____ / ____ / ____

My Daily Journal ____ / ____ / ____

My Daily Journal ____ / ____ / ____

My Daily Journal ____ / ____ / ____

My Daily Journal ____ / ____ / ____

My Daily Journal _____ / _____ / _____

My Daily Journal ____ /____ / ____

My Daily Journal ____ / ____ / ____

My Daily Journal ____ / ____ / ____

My Daily Journal ____ / ____ / ____

My Daily Journal ____ /____ / ____

My Daily Journal ____ / ____ / ____

My Daily Journal ____ /_____ / _____

My Daily Journal ____ /_____ / _____

My Daily Journal ____ / ____ / ____

My Daily Journal ____ / ____ / ____

My Daily Journal ____ / ____ / ____

My Daily Journal ____ / ____ / ____

My Daily Journal ____ /_____ / _____

My Daily Journal ____ / ____ / ____

My Daily Journal ____ / ____ / ____

My Daily Journal ____ / ____ / ____

My Daily Journal ____ /____ / ____

My Daily Journal ____ / ____ / ____

My Daily Journal ____ / ____ / ____

A Washington, DC native JaNeise Sturdivant attends Faith United Ministries in District Heights, Maryland, where her parents, J.E. & P.D. Sturdivant, are the pastors. For more than 20 years, Faith United Ministries has served northeast DC as well as District Heights, MD through community revitalization, family building activities, outreach, and consistent spiritual direction.

Not only is JaNeise a minister and a motivational speaker, but she is also a mentor, activist, and coach who has dedicated herself to empowering youth both spiritually and emotionally. JaNeise is extremely passionate about developing our youth and presenting them with the best opportunities possible. With that in mind, she has created tools to prepare them for their future, ensure they develop a healthy and positive mindset, and equip them to succeed. She is called to help at-risk youth and young adults achieve wholeness through teaching sessions and creating an outlet for positive emotional expression. JaNeise is also the Owner and Manager of JESIEN MENTOR & MODEL PROGRAM, where she provides youth with an array of techniques and teachings that catapults their self-esteem to a higher level.

JaNeise has over 20 years of experience as a Youth Instructor, Fashion Model, Mentor, and Motivational Speaker. Her purpose and assignment are about taking YOU to a higher level of readiness by putting GOD first, self-esteem building, and providing support and opportunities to improve personal growth through life skills.

To book JaNeise for your next event or to connect with her on social media visit the following:

Website - www.jesienmdmgt.com/

Email - jsturdivant2@gmail.com

Instagram - janeise_sturdivant

Facebook - JaNeise Sturdivant

Twitter - @sweetJaNeise

www.ingramcontent.com/pod-product-compliance
Lightning Source LLC
Chambersburg PA
CBHW081118080526
44587CB00021B/3649